BIG BLISS BLUEPRINT WORKBOOK

THE ESSENTIAL COMPANION TO CREATING YOUR BLISS

SHELL PHELPS

Positive Streak Publishing
P.O. Box 575
Pinckney, MI 48169

ISBN: 978-1-7345784-3-0 (print)

Contact Information:
For details email at phelpsstrategies@gmail.com,
website: www.phelpsconsulting.net
to sign up for our Free Newsletter
or call us at (734) 845-2469

Introduction

From the author that brought you the popular book the *Big Bliss Blueprint,* Shell Phelps has fashioned the ultimate workbook, so you can construct your own big bliss blueprint layout.

If you are looking to schedule a personal strategy session, please visit her website at *phelpsconsulting.net*. By clicking on the "Coaching" page, you will see the available appointment options, pricing, and scheduling your own private session made easy right on the site.

For professional groups seeking to schedule Shell for a speaking engagement, in-person or virtual, please email her team at the address below or feel free to call at 734-845-2469.

Enjoyed any part of the book or workbook? Please be kind and share your thoughtful review directly on your favorite bookstore platform to help others find their big bliss.

To sign up for the free newsletter, please visit the website at *phelpsconsulting.net* to register where you can also find all the available social media links.

If you wish to send positive feedback, blissful stories or have questions, please do not hesitate to reach out to the team at Phelps Strategies via email at *phelpsstrategies@gmail.com*. They would like to hear from you.

Keep sharing and building your BLISS!

Contents

How to Use This Workbook

The basics

The fundamental basis of the *Big Bliss Blueprint Workbook* is combining two tactical components. The first is utilizing the original strategies presented in The *Big Bliss Blueprint* book, which is deliberately divided into eight self-guided themed sections. The second is using this workbook for self-reflective journaling and to capture thought responses for reinforcement.

First Step

You will begin by surfing through the 100 strategies offered in each of the eight subdivided sections of the *Big Bliss Blueprint* original book. Select your four favorite strategies within each of the divided categories that inspire your free-flow reflection journaling pages. You'll simply write down your positive thoughts and journal any shifts in perspectives gained from your four hand-picked strategies that resonate with you the most.

Purpose

The purpose of placing an emphasis on your four favorite strategies in each subdivided section is to practice narrowing your focus of thought and to reinforce your positive commitment to them in writing. The written words become intentional and purposeful by the action of writing and memory engagement. You may want to use a pencil to reuse this workbook.

Second Step

Move forward by completing the Strategy Reinforcement Challenges in each themed section. It's critical not to contemplate your answers for longer than five minutes. The first thought is typically the most meaningful. It's also most impactful if you do these challenges on different days.

Day 1 = Focus
Day 2 = Remember
Day 3 = Practice

How to Use This Workbook

Third Step

You will narrow your focus by gravitating towards your favorite strategies and/or impactful lessons learned in the Strategy Reinforcement Challenges in each of the eight themed sections. Create a condensed summary of the enlightened aspects at the end of each section. These eight associated themed room summaries will guide you in forming your Big Bliss Blueprint final layout.

Purpose

Narrowing your focus is learning to filter your thoughts, which is a critical step to the process. The sifting of your thoughts will aid in capturing a visual word diagram or map for your final blueprint at the end of the workbook. Gain clarity by getting rid of the distractions that detract you from obtaining your big bliss. Committing to specific word visualization ropes together your life's map and offers direction.

Fourth Step

To finalize your blueprint, you will refine your focus even narrower by referring to each of the room design section summaries on the last page of each themed section. Zoom-in or craft three words to translate a likeness to each section to configure your final blueprint at the end of the workbook.

Purpose

Shine the light on the most valuable aspect in each section by highlighting key words that bring clarity to your journey to happiness. This is not a workbook that you'll want to blast through. True mindfulness, contemplation, and dedication is walking through each step which will give you the biggest impact.

1

SMALL REFLECTIONS THAT PAY LOVING COMPOUND INTEREST

Read the first section of *The Big Bliss Blueprint* for inspiration to answer the questions in this section.

Reference the 11 themed strategies

The Big Bliss Blueprint Original Book Reference

Strategy Surfing for Free-Flow Reflection

Section 1: Small Reflections That Pay Compound Interest

Page#: ____________________ Date: ____________________

Strategy Name: ____

Theme: Love & Kindness

The Big Bliss Blueprint Original Book Reference

Strategy Surfing for Free-Flow Reflection

Section 1: Small Reflections That Pay Compound Interest

Page#: ____________________ Date: ____________________

Strategy Name: ____

Theme: Love & Kindness

The Big Bliss Blueprint Original Book Reference
Strategy Surfing for Free-Flow Reflection

Section 1: Small Reflections That Pay Compound Interest

Page#: ____________________ Date: ____________________

Strategy Name: ____

____

____

____

____

____

____

____

____

____

____

____

____

____

____

____

____

Theme: Love & Kindness

The Big Bliss Blueprint Original Book Reference

Strategy Surfing for Free-Flow Reflection

Section 1: Small Reflections That Pay Compound Interest

Page#: ____________________ Date: ____________________

Strategy Name: ____

Theme: Love & Kindness

STRATEGY REINFORCEMENT CHALLENGE #1
Small Reflections That Pay Compound Interest

Day 1: Focus – Part One (A)

Date:______________________________

Focus on the first (3) three people who immediately come to your mind and write them down here. The only criteria is these people are currently on your mind. Second, describe the last interaction you had with each person.

*1.*____

(Name & Relationship)

*Last interaction:*______________________________________

____

*2.*____

(Name & Relationship)

*Last interaction:*______________________________________

____

*3.*____

(Name & Relationship)

*Last interaction:*______________________________________

____

Theme: Love & Kindness

STRATEGY REINFORCEMENT CHALLENGE #1

Small Reflections That Pay Compound Interest

Day 1: Focus – Part One (B)

Put extra effort into each person listed and do one thing that makes them feel special. Make their day brighter with a small gesture, special text, email, or call to show them you are thinking of them. Reconnect or enhance the connection in a unique way. Be creative.

FIRST - Person listed from Part One (A):

1. Name:__________________________ Date: ________________

2. Specific effort made: ___________________________________

   ____

   ____

3. Reaction received: _____________________________________

   ____

   ____

4. ☐ Positive ☐ Neutral ☐ Hard to read
   ☐ No Reaction ☐ Disappointed ☐ Negative

5. Your takeaway: _______________________________________

   ____

   ____

   ____

Theme: Love & Kindness

STRATEGY REINFORCEMENT CHALLENGE #1

Small Reflections That Pay Compound Interest

Day 1: Focus – Part One (B) Continued

Put extra effort into each person listed and do one thing that makes them feel special. Make their day brighter with a small gesture, special text, email, or call to show them you are thinking of them. Reconnect or enhance the connection in a unique way. Be creative.

SECOND - Person listed from Part One (A):

1. Name:__________________________ Date: __________________

2. Specific effort made: ____________________________________

____

____

3. Reaction received: ______________________________________

____

____

4. ☐ Positive ☐ Neutral ☐ Hard to read

   ☐ No Reaction ☐ Disappointed ☐ Negative

5. Your takeaway: ____

____

____

____

STRATEGY REINFORCEMENT CHALLENGE #1

Small Reflections That Pay Compound Interest

Day 1: Focus – Part One (B) Continued

Put extra effort into each person listed and do one thing that makes them feel special. Make their day brighter with a small gesture, special text, email, or call to show them you are thinking of them. Reconnect or enhance the connection in a unique way. Be creative.

THIRD - Person listed from Part One (A):

1. Name:________________________ Date: ________________

2. Specific effort made: ______________________________

____

____

3. Reaction received: ________________________________

____

____

4. ☐ Positive ☐ Neutral ☐ Hard to read
☐ No Reaction ☐ Disappointed ☐ Negative

5. Your takeaway: _________________________________

____

____

____

Theme: Love & Kindness

STRATEGY REINFORCEMENT CHALLENGE #1

Small Reflections That Pay Compound Interest

Day 2: Remember

Remember to laugh each day. Challenge yourself to find the humor in something daily. Before you start your day, look for three things that you find humorous (even if only in thought) or at least something that made you smile. Write it down and date it with who, what, and where.

Experience <u>ONE</u>:

1. Who: ______________________________ Date: ______________

2. What happened: ____

____

____

____

3. Where : ____

____

____

4. Positive takeaway: ____________________________________

____

____

____

Theme: Love & Kindness

Day 2: Remember (Continued)

Remember to laugh each day. Challenge yourself to find the humor in something daily. Before you start your day, look for three things that you find humorous (even if only in thought) or at least something that made you smile. Write it down and date it with who, what, and where.

Experience TWO:

1. Who: ____________________________ Date: ______________

2. What happened: _____________________________________

____

____

____

3. Where: ____

____

____

4. Positive takeaway: __________________________________

____

____

____

Theme: Love & Kindness

Day 2: Remember (Continued)

Remember to laugh each day. Challenge yourself to find the humor in something daily. Before you start your day, look for three things that you find humorous (even if only in thought) or at least something that made you smile. Write it down and date it with who, what, and where.

Experience THREE:

1. Who: ______________________ Date: ___________

2. What happened: ______________________________

____

____

____

3. Where: ______________________________

____

____

4. Positive takeaway: ______________________________

____

____

____

Theme: Love & Kindness

STRATEGY REINFORCEMENT CHALLENGE #1
Small Reflections That Pay Compound Interest

Day 3: Practice - Part One (A)

Think of one person you admire. Write a list of the top ten attributes that you admire about that person. Determine which qualities you have that are the same. The unchecked items will be the attributes that will be transferred to the next page.

Admired Person:____________________ Date:__________

<u>*Step One,*</u> list most admired qualities below first

<u>*Step Two,*</u> check active matching attributes

<u>*Step Three,*</u> leave attributes to adopt unchecked

1. ____ ☐
2. ____ ☐
3. ____ ☐
4. ____ ☐
5. ____ ☐
6. ____ ☐
7. ____ ☐
8. ____ ☐
9. ____ ☐
10. ____ ☐

Theme: Love & Kindness

STRATEGY REINFORCEMENT CHALLENGE #1

Small Reflections That Pay Compound Interest

Day 3: Practice - Part One (B)

Transfer the identified qualities (unchecked attributes) you would like to adopt from the previous page. Rank them in order of importance to you below. The top three attributes (A) will become your area of focus.

Admired Person: ____________________ Date: ____________

#1. (A) ____

#2. (A) ____

#3. (A) ____

4. ____

5. ____

6. ____

7. ____

8. ____

9. ____

10. ____

Theme: Love & Kindness

STRATEGY REINFORCEMENT CHALLENGE #1

Small Reflections That Pay Compound Interest

Day 3: Practice - Part Two

Focus on the **FIRST** of the top three attributes you want to adopt from the previous page. Begin practicing and record the outcome below. Journal this challenge.

After adopting the top three qualities, you should continue this work with the rest of the unchecked attributes.

Admired person using as example:________________________

Quality Adopting: ______________________________________

____

Describe the practice scenario outcome:__________________

____

____

____

Experience Takeaway:____________________________________

____

____

____

☐ Positive ☐ Neutral ☐ Need more practice

☐ Negative ☐ Disappointed ☐ Not too bad

Theme: Love & Kindness

STRATEGY REINFORCEMENT CHALLENGE #1

Small Reflections That Pay Compound Interest

Day 3: Practice - Part Two

Focus on the **SECOND** of the top three attributes you want to adopt from the previous page. Begin practicing and record the outcome below. Journal this challenge.

After adopting the top three qualities, you should continue this work with the rest of the unchecked attributes.

Admired person using as example:______________________________

Quality Adopting :____

____

Describe the practice scenario outcome:______________________

____

____

____

Experience Takeaway:____

____

____

____

☐ Positive ☐ Neutral ☐ Need more practice

☐ Negative ☐ Disappointed ☐ Not too bad

Theme: Love & Kindness

STRATEGY REINFORCEMENT CHALLENGE #1

Small Reflections That Pay Compound Interest

Day 3: Practice - Part Two

Focus on the **THIRD** of the top three attributes you want to adopt from the previous page. Begin practicing and record the outcome below. Journal this challenge.

After adopting the top three qualities, you should continue this work with the rest of the unchecked attributes.

Admired person using as example: ______________________________

Quality Adopting: ____

____

Describe the practice scenario outcome: ________________________

____

____

____

Experience Takeaway: ____

____

____

____

- ☐ Positive
- ☐ Neutral
- ☐ Need more practice
- ☐ Negative
- ☐ Disappointed
- ☐ Not too bad

Theme: Love & Kindness

Room design #1 of Your Big Bliss Blueprint Layout

Section 1: Small Reflections That Pay Compound Interest

Write a condensed conclusion below based on any lessons learned, a main point, or key message that brought you further understanding or clarity from this section's experience or observations. This is called narrowing your focus. The more concise, the better.

Love & Kindness

What inspiration brought you clarity in this themed section?

2 WHEN THE NEEDS OF ONE OUTWEIGH THE NEEDS OF MANY

Read the second section of *The Big Bliss Blueprint* for inspiration to answer the questions in this section.

Reference the 12 themed strategies

The Big Bliss Blueprint Original Book Reference

Strategy Surfing for Free-Flow Reflection

Section 2: When the Needs of One Outweigh the Needs of Many

Page#: ____________________ Date: ____________________

Strategy Name: ____

____

____

____

____

____

____

____

____

____

____

____

____

____

____

____

____

Theme: Putting Yourself First

The Big Bliss Blueprint Original Book Reference

Strategy Surfing for Free-Flow Reflection

Section 2: When the Needs of One Outweigh the Needs of Many

Page#: ____________________ Date: ____________________

Strategy Name: ____

____

____

____

____

____

____

____

____

____

____

____

____

____

____

____

____

Theme: Putting Yourself First

The Big Bliss Blueprint Original Book Reference

Strategy Surfing for Free-Flow Reflection

Section 2: When the Needs of One Outweigh the Needs of Many

Page#: ____________________ Date: ____________________

Strategy Name: ____

____

____

____

____

____

____

____

____

____

____

____

____

____

____

____

____

Theme: Putting Yourself First

The Big Bliss Blueprint Original Book Reference

Strategy Surfing for Free-Flow Reflection

Section 2: When the Needs of One Outweigh the Needs of Many

Page#: ____________________ Date: ____________________

Strategy Name: ____

____

____

____

____

____

____

____

____

____

____

____

____

____

____

____

____

Theme: Putting Yourself First

STRATEGY REINFORCEMENT CHALLENGE #2

When the Needs of One Outweigh the Needs of Many

Day 1: Focus

Focus on giving yourself permission to enjoy life. Unplug, go outside, go for a drive, go to a beach or lake, do whatever it takes to relax. Focus on having some *"ME"* time. Challenge yourself to do this once a week by giving yourself permission to have fun. Create this habit to rejuvenate. Add to your weekly calendar and slowly increase the duration without any electronic devices.

First Scheduled Attempt

Unplugged activity:____

____

Date: ___________________ Day of Week: ___________________

Length of *"Me"* time: ___________________________________

(full day, ½ Day, # hour(s), or # minutes)

Unplugged Outcome: ☐ Successful ☐ Tempted ☐ Struggled ☐ Difficult ☐ Unsuccessful

Takeaway: ____

____

What would you do differently next time: ___________________

____

____

Theme: Putting Yourself First

STRATEGY REINFORCEMENT CHALLENGE #2

When the Needs of One Outweigh the Needs of Many

Day 1: Focus (Continued)

Focus on giving yourself permission to enjoy life. Unplug, go outside, go for a drive, go to a beach or lake, do whatever it takes to relax. Focus on having some "*ME*" time. Challenge yourself to do this once a week by giving yourself permission to have fun. Create this habit to rejuvenate. Add to your weekly calendar and slowly increase the duration without any electronic devices.

Second Scheduled Attempt

Unplugged activity:______________________________________

____

Date: ____________________ Day of Week:____________________

Length of "*Me*" time: ______________________________
(full day, ½ Day, # hour(s), or # minutes)

Unplugged Outcome: ☐ Successful ☐ Tempted
☐ Struggled ☐ Difficult ☐ Unsuccessful

Takeaway:____

____

What would you do differently next time: ___________________

____

____

Theme: Putting Yourself First

STRATEGY REINFORCEMENT CHALLENGE #2

When the Needs of One Outweigh the Needs of Many

Day 2: Remember

When stressed, practice shifting gears. Redirect your thoughts and replace them with new nouns (people, places, or things) that give you positive input. Read, go for a walk, watch TV, or hang out with someone. Remember that your thoughts are a direct link to your perception and attitude. Redirect yourself.

Date:________________________Stressor:___________________

____

Redirection used:____

_______________________________ person(s) place, or thing(s)

Strategy(s) & Page(s) used as support: _____________________

____

____

Redirected thought used with success: ____________________

____

____

Redirection Outcome: ☐ Successful ☐ Improvement ☐ Struggled ☐ Difficult ☐ Unsuccessful

Takeaway:____

____

____

Theme: Putting Yourself First

STRATEGY REINFORCEMENT CHALLENGE #2

When the Needs of One Outweigh the Needs of Many

Day 3: Practice

If you could change one thing about yourself, what would it be? Why would you change it? What stops you from making this change? Create the rationale to make it happen or ask for help. Look for small ways to take action to be your best self. You're the only one who can. Alter only *one* change at a time until it becomes part of you.

Date:______________________________

Desired change:____

____

____

Reason for change: ____

____

____

Obstacle(s) to change:____

____

____

Support Person(s) : ____

Describe help needed:____

____

____

Theme: Putting Yourself First

Room design #2 of Your Big Bliss Blueprint Layout

Section 2: When the Needs of One Outweigh the Needs of Many

Write a condensed conclusion below based on any lessons learned, a main point, or key message that brought you further understanding or clarity from this section's experience or observations. This is called narrowing your focus. The more concise, the better.

Putting Yourself First

What inspiration brought you clarity in this themed section?

3 EACH CONNECTION LENDS TO A VAST NETWORK

Read the third section of *The Big Bliss Blueprint* for inspiration to answer the questions in this section.

Reference the 11 themed strategies

Strategy Surfing for Free-Flow Reflection

Section 3: Each Connection Lends to a Vast Network

Page#: ____________________ Date: ____________________

Strategy Name: ______________________________________

Theme: Relationships

The Big Bliss Blueprint Original Book Reference

Strategy Surfing for Free-Flow Reflection

Section 3: Each Connection Lends to a Vast Network

Page#: ____________________ Date: ____________________

Strategy Name: ____

Theme: Relationships

The Big Bliss Blueprint Original Book Reference

Strategy Surfing for Free-Flow Reflection

Section 3: Each Connection Lends to a Vast Network

Page#: ____________________ Date: ____________________

Strategy Name: ______________________________________

Theme: Relationships

The Big Bliss Blueprint Original Book Reference

Strategy Surfing for Free-Flow Reflection

Section 3: Each Connection Lends to a Vast Network

Page#: ____________________ Date: ____________________

Strategy Name: ____

Theme: Relationships

STRATEGY REINFORCEMENT CHALLENGE #3

Each Connection Lends to a Vast Network

Day 1: Focus

Focus on not complaining in your daily conversations. Focus on *what's right* or the good in situations and bypass the *what's wrong* topics. You'll notice others will follow your lead and conversations will be more positive, naturally. Be the one who sees what's right instead of what's wrong.

Date:____________________________

Describe a challenging event:____________________________________

____

____

What was right or good:____

____

____

Negative topic Bypassed: ______________________________________

____

____

Refraining Results: ☐ Successful ☐ Improvement

☐ Struggled ☐ Difficult ☐ Unsuccessful

Takeaway: ____

____

____

Theme: Relationships

STRATEGY REINFORCEMENT CHALLENGE #3

Each Connection Lends to a Vast Network

Day 2: Remember – Part One

As you interact with others in your life, remember to start taking inventory. Are the people closest to you the people with whom you want to surround yourself? If someone is high maintenance (*HM*) consistently, consider a *fade* (taking a short break from interacting) if it's becoming intolerable.

First, list the 10 people closest to you. Second, go back and check the boxes that apply to each person. The individuals with both boxes checked indicate it's time to re-evaluate.

1. ______________________________ ☐ HM ☐ Fade
2. ______________________________ ☐ HM ☐ Fade
3. ______________________________ ☐ HM ☐ Fade
4. ______________________________ ☐ HM ☐ Fade
5. ______________________________ ☐ HM ☐ Fade
6. ______________________________ ☐ HM ☐ Fade
7. ______________________________ ☐ HM ☐ Fade
8. ______________________________ ☐ HM ☐ Fade
9. ______________________________ ☐ HM ☐ Fade
10. ______________________________ ☐ HM ☐ Fade

Theme: Relationships

STRATEGY REINFORCEMENT CHALLENGE #3

Each Connection Lends to a Vast Network

Day 2: Remember – Part 2

Is there anyone you would consider *fading* (allowing time to pass between interactions)? If yes, indicate _one_ person below. Consider heavily the rationale for a temporary fade for a more limited relationship. I recommend fading only one person at a time to allow the ability to assess the space they leave behind.

Write the name of a person you would consider fading below:

1. ______________________________ Years Known _______________

Specific reason(s): ____

____

____

____

____

2. Specific length of fade time ________________________________

____

If you do decide to fade a person, set a specific length of time to allow yourself some space to reduce or limit interactions.
The goal is _*NOT*_ to ignore that person, that would be hurtful.

Be honest whenever possible. Sometimes space brings clarity. Take the time you need to re-evaluate the relationship to determine the level of closeness in the relationship then have the conversation. If no fading is necessary, skip this page.

Theme: Relationships

STRATEGY REINFORCEMENT CHALLENGE #3

Each Connection Lends to a Vast Network

Day 2: Remember – Part 3

Record the results from *fading* below by indicating how much time actually passed versus the estimated time. Consider if further fading is desired or if it's time for that one-on-one conversation. Give careful consideration for clarity. Ask yourself if this person brings moments of bliss to your life?

Transfer the name of the one person faded below:

1. ______________________________

Actual Duration: ______________________________

Feelings during fading: ______________________________

____

____

____

____

____

2. Did you find yourself of missing this person? ☐ Yes ☐ NO

Explain: ______________________________

____

____

____

____

Theme: Relationships

STRATEGY REINFORCEMENT CHALLENGE #3

Each Connection Lends to a Vast Network

Day 2: Remember – Part 4

We should add value to each other's lives. Some people are in our lives for a short period to teach us lessons as we grow. Reflect on a past or current person that faded from your life.

Write the name of one person you faded below:

1.____

What moments of bliss did they bring to your life? __________

____

____

____

____

____

____

____

____

____

____

____

Fading opens space for the next person. While some friendships last a lifetime, others will naturally drift away but everyone in our lives still leaves a trail.

Theme: Relationships

STRATEGY REINFORCEMENT CHALLENGE #3

Each Connection Lends to a Vast Network

Day 3: Practice

Think of that one person who irritates you the most. Now think of three positive attributes or skills this person has. Yes, you can. Dig deep. All people have talents, but generally, it's a personality clash that may cause you to dislike someone. This exercise is pivotal for self-growth.

Name: ______________________________ Date: ______________

How do you know this person?________________________________

____

#1 Positive Skill/attribute: __________________________________

____

____

#2 Positive Skill/attribute:___________________________________

____

____

#2 Positive Skill/attribute:___________________________________

____

____

Although you can't change that person, you can change your perspective of them by observing another side of them. If you completed this challenge, I'm so proud of you!

Theme: Relationships

Room design #3 of Your Big Bliss Blueprint Layout

Section 3: Each Connection Lends to a Vast Network

Write a condensed conclusion below based on any lessons learned, a main point, or key message that brought you further understanding or clarity from this section's experience or observations. This is called narrowing your focus. The more concise, the better.

Relationships

What inspiration brought you clarity in this themed section?

4 A WHISPER IN THE MOMENT CAN ECHO THROUGH A LIFETIME

Read the fourth section of *The Big Bliss Blueprint* for inspiration to answer the questions in this section.

Reference the 13 themed strategies

The Big Bliss Blueprint Original Book Reference

Strategy Surfing for Free-Flow Reflection

Section 4: A Whisper in the Moment Can Echo through a Lifetime

Page#: ____________________ Date: ____________________

Strategy Name: ____

Theme: Communication

Strategy Surfing for Free-Flow Reflection

Section 4: A Whisper in the Moment Can Echo through a Lifetime

Page#: ____________________ Date: ____________________

Strategy Name: ____

Theme: Communication

The Big Bliss Blueprint Original Book Reference

Strategy Surfing for Free-Flow Reflection

Section 4: A Whisper in the Moment Can Echo through a Lifetime

Page#: ____________________ Date: ____________________

Strategy Name: ____

____

____

____

____

____

____

____

____

____

____

____

____

____

____

____

____

Theme: Communication

The Big Bliss Blueprint Original Book Reference

Strategy Surfing for Free-Flow Reflection

Section 4: A Whisper in the Moment Can Echo through a Lifetime

Page#: ____________________ Date: ____________________

Strategy Name: ____

____

____

____

____

____

____

____

____

____

____

____

____

____

____

____

____

Theme: Communication

STRATEGY REINFORCEMENT CHALLENGE #4

A Whisper in the Moment Can Echo through a Lifetime

Day 1: Focus

Focus on the content of your message. Ask yourself what your message is and what impression you want your audience to be left with at the end of the conversation or communication. Focus on a challenging situation to help filter and create a mindful message:

1. What is the intent (goal) of your message or conversation?

____

____

____

2. What impression do you want to leave with this person(s)?

____

____

____

3. How will you know the interaction was successful?

____

____

____

Focus on massaging your thoughts before delivery to be a mindful messenger. Be intentional with your words. If your message is unclear, the receiver will be left to decipher it.

Theme: Communication

STRATEGY REINFORCEMENT CHALLENGE #4

A Whisper in the Moment Can Echo through a Lifetime

Day 2: Remember

Remember that it's fine to decline. Saying no can be challenging but it's all in the approach. Be confident and kind when saying it. "I'll catch you next time" or "I would love to, but I have plans" are good examples of declining gracefully. Pre-design your "No thanks" statements and keep them in your back pocket.

1.What situation is the most difficult for you to say "No?" _____

____

____

____

2. Why do you find it difficult? ______________________

____

____

____

3. Pre-plan ways to decline gracefully: _______________

____

____

____

____

Remember to practice saying no to less challenging situations and work your way up to your biggest ones. It gets easier!

Theme: Communication

STRATEGY REINFORCEMENT CHALLENGE #4

A Whisper in the Moment Can Echo through a Lifetime

Day 3: Practice

Practice challenging yourself with previous missed messages. Reflect on a recent conversation in which your message was misinterpreted because it was unclear to the receiver.

1. Identify part of a conversation where you had a missed message. What did you make unclear? ____________________

    ____

    ____

    ____

    ____

2. Rewrite your missed message here to give it more clarity:

    ____

    ____

    ____

    ____

    ____

    ____

    ____

See this as an opportunity to recraft a new delivery. What would you do next time to convey a better and more mindful message? Practice often!

Theme: Communication

Room design #4 of Your Big Bliss Blueprint Layout

Section 4: A Whisper in the Moment Can Echo through a Lifetime

Write a condensed conclusion below based on any lessons learned, a main point, or key message that brought you further understanding or clarity from this section's experience or observations. This is called narrowing your focus. The more concise, the better.

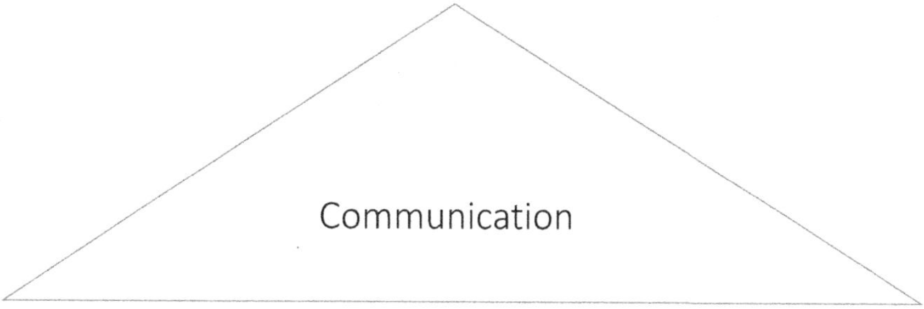

What inspiration brought you clarity in this themed section?

5 SEEDS OF AMBITION ARE THE FRUIT OF SUCCESS

Read the fifth section of *The Big Bliss Blueprint* for inspiration to answer the questions in this section.

Reference the 14 themed strategies

Section 5: Seeds of Ambition Are the Fruit of Success

Page#: ____________________ Date: ____________________

Strategy Name: ____

____

____

____

____

____

____

____

____

____

____

____

____

____

____

____

____

Theme: Goal-Setting

Section 5: Seeds of Ambition Are the Fruit of Success

Page#: ____________________ Date: ____________________

Strategy Name: ____

____

____

____

____

____

____

____

____

____

____

____

____

____

____

____

____

Theme: Goal-Setting

Strategy Surfing for Free-Flow Reflection

Section 5: Seeds of Ambition Are the Fruit of Success

Page#: ____________________ Date: ____________________

Strategy Name: ____

Theme: Goal-Setting

Strategy Surfing for Free-Flow Reflection

Section 5: Seeds of Ambition Are the Fruit of Success

Page#: ____________________ Date: ____________________

Strategy Name: ____

____

____

____

____

____

____

____

____

____

____

____

____

____

____

____

____

Theme: Goal-Setting

STRATEGY REINFORCEMENT CHALLENGE #5

Seeds of Ambition Are the Fruit of Success

Day 1: Focus

Setting goals starts with focusing on your top three goals. Having too many goals lead to uncompleted goals. What's most important? Then decide your next step for each goal. Focus on what *needs* to be done versus what you *want* to do. Use this method as a filter for your next action steps.

List below your top three goals:

#1. ____

____

Next action step:________________________________

____

#2. ____

____

Next action step:________________________________

____

#3. ____

____

Next action step: ________________________________

____

Prioritizing your goals is key to achievement and focus. Knowing your next course of action brings you one step closer to obtaining each goal.

Theme: Goal-Setting

STRATEGY REINFORCEMENT CHALLENGE #5

Seeds of Ambition Are the Fruit of Success

Day 2: Remember

Remember that if you get stuck while attaining a goal, make a step-by-step plan by breaking down the goal into smaller tasks. Get support if it causes you to feel overwhelmed. Remember to work on one goal at a time and start with the one that will have the most impact. Get unstuck, revise your plan. Move forward!

Which goals from the previous page will be the most

challenging? ____

____

What make it more challenging? ______________________

____

____

____

If you get stuck, what or who will be your resource or

support person(s) for help?____________________________

____

____

____

Knowing what to do ahead of time to get you unstuck helps keep you moving forward because you will already know what you'll do next.

Theme: Goal-Setting

STRATEGY REINFORCEMENT CHALLENGE #5

Seeds of Ambition Are the Fruit of Success

Day 3: Practice

Practice staying in the positive zone. Think of one thing you're grateful for daily. It is impossible to feel grateful and unhappy at the same time. Shift your thoughts onto what you can do versus what you can't do.

Date this challenge:________________________________

What is one thing your grateful for today?______________

____

____

____

Identify one thing you can do today for one of your goals:

____

____

____

Look for the positive in a bad situation and find the positive outcome: ________________________________

____

____

____

____

Theme: Goal-Setting

Room design #5 of Your Big Bliss Blueprint Layout

Section 5: Seeds of Ambition Are the Fruit of Success

Write a condensed conclusion below based on any lessons learned, a main point, or key message that brought you further understanding or clarity from this section's experience or observations. This is called narrowing your focus. The more concise, the better.

What inspiration brought you clarity in this themed section?

6

A GOOD CHOICE NOW LAYS THE FOUNDATION OF PROSPERITY

Read the sixth section of *The Big Bliss Blueprint* for inspiration to answer the questions in this section.

Reference the 12 themed strategies

The Big Bliss Blueprint Original Book Reference

Strategy Surfing for Free-Flow Reflection

Section 6: A Good Choice Now Lays the Foundation of Prosperity

Page#: ____________________ Date: ____________________

Strategy Name: ____

Theme: Decision-Making

The Big Bliss Blueprint Original Book Reference

Strategy Surfing for Free-Flow Reflection

Section 6: A Good Choice Now Lays the Foundation of Prosperity

Page#: ____________________ Date: ____________________

Strategy Name: ____

Theme: Decision-Making

The Big Bliss Blueprint Original Book Reference

Strategy Surfing for Free-Flow Reflection

Section 6: A Good Choice Now Lays the Foundation of Prosperity

Page#: ____________________ Date: ____________________

Strategy Name: ______________________________________

Theme: Decision-Making

The Big Bliss Blueprint Original Book Reference

Strategy Surfing for Free-Flow Reflection

Section 6: A Good Choice Now Lays the Foundation of Prosperity

Page#: ____________________ Date: ____________________

Strategy Name: ____

Theme: Decision-Making

STRATEGY REINFORCEMENT CHALLENGE #6

A Good Choice Now Lays the Foundation of Prosperity

Day 1: Focus

Focus on aligning your priorities with the three goals you identified in Strategy Reinforcement Challenge #5.
Rank your three goals below in order of importance. If your priorities and goals don't align, revise your goals here until they match. Stay focused and make decisions to work toward your goals and the meaning behind each one.

#1. ______________________________

What will it mean to achieve this goal:______________

____

____

____

#2. ______________________________

What will it mean to achieve this goal:______________

____

____

____

#3.______________________________

What will it mean to achieve this goal:______________

____

____

Theme: Decision-Making

STRATEGY REINFORCEMENT CHALLENGE #6

A Good Choice Now Lays the Foundation of Prosperity

Day 2: Remember – Part One

Remember that you're in charge of your schedule but you can't do it all. Goals are great to achieve but make sure to enjoy the journey. Carve out some "ME" time. Select a day and a few hours to set aside on your calendar to relax. Do one fun thing a week at a minimum or rest for a couple of hours without being productive. Make this a habit.

Select the day, time, and duration below.

Example: [X] *Sunday* ___*3:00*___ *A.M. or P.M.* ___*2*___ *hr(s).*

1. [ ] Monday ________ A.M. or P.M. ________hr(s.)

2. [ ] Tuesday ________ A.M. or P.M. ________hr(s.)

3. [ ] Wednesday ________ A.M. or P.M. ________hr(s.)

4. [ ] Thursday ________ A.M. or P.M. ________hr(s.)

5. [ ] Friday ________ A.M. or P.M. ________hr(s.)

6. [ ] Saturday ________ A.M. or P.M. ________hr(s.)

7. [ ] Sunday ________ A.M. or P.M. ________hr(s.)

Make this commitment to yourself and transfer this "ME" appointment to your calendar weekly.

Theme: Decision-Making

STRATEGY REINFORCEMENT CHALLENGE #6

A Good Choice Now Lays the Foundation of Prosperity

Day 2: Remember – Part Two

Describe the event(s) of your scheduled "ME" date with yourself.

How much time did you carve out of your day?__________

____

How did you spend your "ME" time? ________________

____

____

____

____

Describe your experience and your ability to relax_______

____

____

____

____

When is your next "ME" date and your plans:__________

____

____

____

Theme: Decision-Making

STRATEGY REINFORCEMENT CHALLENGE #6

A Good Choice Now Lays the Foundation of Prosperity

Day 3: Practice

Practice making decisions that make you feel comfortable. It's wonderful to have solid expectations but make room for some flexibility. Incorporate being adaptable while identifying what is most important. Practice filling in the blank.

Is it more important to ________________________________

than to ________________________________?

Example:
Is it more important to **eat ice cream** than to **eat healthily**?

If your goal is to lose weight, your action does not align with your goal. Don't negotiate with yourself. Respect your goal.

Fill in the blank which decision you struggle making:

Is it more important to ________________________________

____

____

than to____

____

____

____?

Ensure you align your decisions with your goals.

Theme: Decision-Making

Room design #6 of Your Big Bliss Blueprint Layout

Section 6: A Good Choice Now Lays the Foundation of Prosperity

Write a condensed conclusion below based on any lessons learned, a main point, or key message that brought you further understanding or clarity from this section's experience or observations. This is called narrowing your focus. The more concise, the better.

Decision-Making

What inspiration brought you clarity in this themed section?

7

ONE-DEGREE SHIFTS NAVIGATE TO AN AUTHENTIC TRUE SELF

Read the seventh section of *The Big Bliss Blueprint* for inspiration to answer the questions in this section.

Reference the 12 themed strategies

The Big Bliss Blueprint Original Book Reference

Strategy Surfing for Free-Flow Reflection

Section 7: One-Degree Shifts Navigate to an Authentic True Self

Page#: ____________________ Date: ____________________

Strategy Name: ____

____

____

____

____

____

____

____

____

____

____

____

____

____

____

____

____

Theme: Prioritizing Self-Care

The Big Bliss Blueprint Original Book Reference

Strategy Surfing for Free-Flow Reflection

Section 7: One-Degree Shifts Navigate to an Authentic True Self

Page#: ___________________ Date: ____________________

Strategy Name: ______________________________________

____

____

____

____

____

____

____

____

____

____

____

____

____

____

____

____

Theme: Prioritizing Self-Care

Section 7: One-Degree Shifts Navigate to an Authentic True Self

Page#: ____________________ Date: _____________________

Strategy Name: ____

____

____

____

____

____

____

____

____

____

____

____

____

____

____

____

____

Theme: Prioritizing Self-Care

The Big Bliss Blueprint Original Book Reference

Strategy Surfing for Free-Flow Reflection

Section 7: One-Degree Shifts Navigate to an Authentic True Self

Page#: ____________________ Date: ____________________

Strategy Name: ____

____

____

____

____

____

____

____

____

____

____

____

____

____

____

____

____

Theme: Prioritizing Self-Care

STRATEGY REINFORCEMENT CHALLENGE #7

One-Degree Shifts Navigate to an Authentic True Self

Day 1: Focus – Part One; Part A

Focus on bringing more joy to each day. Step one is to list the **people** who keep your spirits up. Write down your initial answers within five minutes. The goal is to bring your daily focus on joy that is not attached to things.

1. ______________________________

2. ______________________________

3. ______________________________

4. ______________________________

5. ______________________________

6. ______________________________

7. ______________________________

8. ______________________________

9. ______________________________

10. ______________________________

Theme: Prioritizing Self-Care

STRATEGY REINFORCEMENT CHALLENGE #7

One-Degree Shifts Navigate to an Authentic True Self

Day 1: Focus - Continue: Part One; Part B

Focus on bringing more joy to each day. Part B is to list the **places** that keep your spirits up. Write down your initial answers within five minutes. The goal is to bring your daily focus on joy that is not attached to things.

1. ______________________________

2. ______________________________

3. ______________________________

4. ______________________________

5. ______________________________

6. ______________________________

7. ______________________________

8. ______________________________

9. ______________________________

10. ______________________________

Theme: Prioritizing Self-Care

STRATEGY REINFORCEMENT CHALLENGE #7

One-Degree Shifts Navigate to an Authentic True Self

Day 1: Focus - Continue: Part Two; Part A

Continue focusing on what brings you joy each day. Select three **people in part one** by ranking them in order. Who brings you the most joy? Step two is to focus on the reasons they create joy for you. Identifying reasons that are not associated with things.

#1. Joyful person: ______________________________

Reason:______________________________________

____

____

____

#2. Joyful person: ______________________________

Reason:______________________________________

____

____

____

#3. Joyful person: ______________________________

Reason: _____________________________________

____

____

____

Theme: Prioritizing Self-Care

STRATEGY REINFORCEMENT CHALLENGE #7

One-Degree Shifts Navigate to an Authentic True Self

Day 1: Focus - Continue: Part Two; Part B

Continue focusing on what brings you joy each day. Relist the top three **places in part one** by ranking them in order. What locations bring you the most joy? Step two is to focus on the reasons why they create joy or comfort for you. It's important to identify joy that is not attached to things.

#1. Joyful place: ________________________________

____

Reason:____

____

____

#2. Joyful place: ________________________________

____

Reason:____

____

____

#3. Joyful place: ________________________________

Reason:____

____

____

Theme: Prioritizing Self-Care

STRATEGY REINFORCEMENT CHALLENGE #7

One-Degree Shifts Navigate to an Authentic True Self

Day 2: Remember

Remember to take care of your needs first. Challenge yourself to do at least one thing for yourself today. It could be as simple as reading a book, walking, or hanging out with friends or family. Depleting yourself of joy may bring emptiness. Enjoy your me-time. Do something you haven't done in a while—just do it!

Put yourself first today and do something just for you and describe what you did below:______________________________

____

____

____

____

Describe the experience with your authentic feelings. Did you enjoy yourself? Did you feel guilty? Describe below: ________

____

____

____

____

____

Set aside another day and time to enjoy another activity. Keep filling your emotional bank account.

Theme: Prioritizing Self-Care

STRATEGY REINFORCEMENT CHALLENGE #7

One-Degree Shifts Navigate to an Authentic True Self

Day 3: Practice – Part One

Practice saying “No” in kind ways to honor your own boundaries. You can’t be everywhere or do everything. If you need space, take it. Without guilt, take care of your own emotional well-being. You don’t owe others an explanation. It’s ok to honor yourself first. Incorporate this into your life regularly.

Identify a topic you struggle with saying “No” and the reason it’s difficult to say “No”. See examples below.

Topic: ______________________________

____

____

____

Reason: ______________________________

____

____

Examples:

Topic: *It’s difficult to say “NO” to a family member who wants to borrow money.*

Reason: *I don’t want to let anyone in my family down. I feel guilty saying “No” even though they keep making poor decisions. I don’t want to hurt their feelings.*

Theme: Prioritizing Self-Care

STRATEGY REINFORCEMENT CHALLENGE #7
One-Degree Shifts Navigate to an Authentic True Self

Day 3: Practice – Part Two

Practice saying "No" in kind ways to honor your own boundaries. Without guilt, take care of your own emotional well-being. You don't owe others an explanation. It's ok to honor yourself first.

Practice saying "No" to the situation described on the previous page that respects your boundaries and is not hurtful to the other person. See examples below.

#1. Practice response:________________________________

____

____

____

#2. Practice response:________________________________

____

____

____

Examples:

#1. Response: *While It's difficult to say "NO" to you, I can't right now*.

#2. (Example) Response: *You know I love and care about you, but it's just something I can't do at this time.*

Theme: Prioritizing Self-Care

Room design #6 of Your Big Bliss Blueprint Layout

Section 7: One-Degree Shifts Navigate to an Authentic True Self

Write a condensed conclusion below based on any lessons learned, a main point, or key message that brought you further understanding or clarity from this section's experience or observations. This is called narrowing your focus. The more concise, the better.

Prioritizing Self-Care

What inspiration brought you clarity in this themed section?

8 MICROSCOPIC THOUGHTS SHAPE YOUR ATMOSPHERE

Read the eighth section of *The Big Bliss Blueprint* for inspiration to answer the questions in this section.

Reference the 12 themed strategies

The Big Bliss Blueprint Original Book Reference

Strategy Surfing for Free-Flow Reflection

Section 8: Microscopic Thoughts Shape Your Atmosphere

Page#: ____________________ Date: ____________________

Strategy Name: ____

Theme: Pulling It All Together

The Big Bliss Blueprint Original Book Reference

Strategy Surfing for Free-Flow Reflection

Section 8: Microscopic Thoughts Shape Your Atmosphere

Page#: ____________________ Date: ____________________

Strategy Name: ____

Theme: Pulling It All Together

The Big Bliss Blueprint Original Book Reference

Strategy Surfing for Free-Flow Reflection

Section 8: Microscopic Thoughts Shape Your Atmosphere

Page#: ____________________ Date: ____________________

Strategy Name: ____

Theme: Pulling It All Together

The Big Bliss Blueprint Original Book Reference

Strategy Surfing for Free-Flow Reflection

Section 8: Microscopic Thoughts Shape Your Atmosphere

Page#: ____________________ Date: ____________________

Strategy Name: ____

Theme: Pulling It All Together

STRATEGY REINFORCEMENT CHALLENGE #8

Microscopic Thoughts Shape Your Atmosphere

Day 1: Focus - Part One

Focus on the details; you may be missing many details daily. Stop, look, listen, and feel what is around you. Notice something new about someone else, yourself, or your surroundings. Write down the details you notice.

Date:__________________ Day of Week:________________

Describe current environment: _________________________

____

____

____

____

____

Close your eyes, what sounds do you hear?_______________

____

____

____

Appreciate the little things that you may take for granted. Continue this challenge on the next page.

Theme: Pulling It All Together

STRATEGY REINFORCEMENT CHALLENGE #8
Microscopic Thoughts Shape Your Atmosphere

Day 1: Focus - Part Two

Focus on the details; you may be missing many details daily. Stop, look, listen, and feel what is around you. Notice something new about someone else, yourself, or your surroundings. Write down the details you notice.

Date:___________________ Day of Week:__________________

How do you feel in this environment? _____________________

____

____

____

Identify all the new detail you hadn't noticed before: ______

____

____

____

____

____

____

Appreciate the little things that you may take for granted.

Theme: Pulling It All Together

STRATEGY REINFORCEMENT CHALLENGE #8
Microscopic Thoughts Shape Your Atmosphere

Day 2: Remember – Part One

Remember to look for those life codes. Do you feel you are on the right path? The signs can be very subtle or glaring right at you, but simply remember to pay attention to them. Did you notice any significant signs?

Date:________________ Day of Week:__________________

1. Describe an area in your life that *is* working well: _____

____

____

____

____

____

2. What signs are you receiving that confirm this? _______

____

____

____

____

____

____

Theme: Pulling It All Together

STRATEGY REINFORCEMENT CHALLENGE #8
Microscopic Thoughts Shape Your Atmosphere

Day 2: Remember – Part Two

Remember to look for those life codes. The signs can be very subtle or glaring right at you, but simply remember to pay attention to them. Did you notice any significant signs indicating an area that is ***NOT*** working in your life?

Date:_______________ Day of Week:_________________

1. Describe an area in your life that is *not* working: ____

____

____

____

____

____

2. What signs indicate this situation is *not* working for you?

____

____

____

____

____

____

STRATEGY REINFORCEMENT CHALLENGE #8

Microscopic Thoughts Shape Your Atmosphere

Day 2: Remember – Part Two Continued

Remember to look for those life codes. The signs can be very subtle or glaring right at you, but simply remember to pay attention to them. Refer to the significant signs listed on the previous page showing you're ***NOT*** *on the* right path.

Date:_______________ Day of Week:_________________

1. What's one change are your willing to make to redirect your course and help to re-align this area? _________

    ____

    ____

    ____

    ____

    ____

2. What signs will you be looking for to know you have successfully redirected your course to the right path?

    ____

    ____

    ____

    ____

    ____

    ____

Theme: Pulling It All Together

STRATEGY REINFORCEMENT CHALLENGE #8

Microscopic Thoughts Shape Your Atmosphere

Day 3: Practice

Practice finding a new opportunity, something that you normally wouldn't do. Reach outside of your comfort zone and discover your growth potential. You may be surprised about what you learn.

Date:_______________ Day of Week:_________________

1. What is one *new* thing you tried this week?__________

____

____

____

____

____

____

2. What did you learn about yourself from the experience?

____

____

____

____

____

____

Room design #6 of Your Big Bliss Blueprint Layout

Section 8: Microscopic Thoughts Shape Your Atmosphere

Write a condensed conclusion below based on any lessons learned, a main point, or key message that brought you further understanding or clarity from this section's experience or observations. This is called narrowing your focus. The more concise, the better.

Pulling It All Together

What inspiration brought you clarity in this themed section?

Your Big Bliss Blueprint Layout

Continue narrowing your focus by condensing your summaries at the end of each section by using a stringent filter. Select one to three words to describe each themed section to define each room below.

1. Love & Kindness

2. Putting Yourself First

3. Relationship Building

4. Communication

5. Goal-setting

6. Decision-Making

7. Prioritizing Self-Care

8. Pulling It Altogether

Final Words of Wisdom

Write your own script. Life can be difficult, but it also has so many wonderful possibilities. If you need a little help or support to navigate life, Phelps Strategies is available. The point is, as a good friend once said to me, "Don't wait and make the world small." In my words, it's your life so make it yours. You will get no second chances. Be your best version of you. Above all, try and stay positive!

Go back and review your workbook journal from the beginning. Take note of the dates and situations. Reread it six months from now. It's funny how much changes in such a short time and what you may have thought was important really wasn't.

For additional information, please visit our website at www.phelpsconsulting.net.

In great gratitude

Shell Phelps, author

Made in the USA
Monee, IL
04 November 2026

67379712R00059